THE
POWDER
ROAD

THE POWDER ROAD

GAVIN CUMMINGS

STEPHAN DRAKE

OSKAR ENANDER

MARK SMITH

STELLAR BOOKS
BOULDER, COLORADO

The Powder Road
© 2005, The Powder Road LLC

Printed in Canada.

10 9 8 7 6 5 4 3 2 1

International Standard Book Number: ISBN 0-9723422-5-7

Library of Congress Cataloging-in-Publication Data

The powder road / Stephan Drake ... [et al.].
   p. cm.
  Includes index.
  ISBN-13: 978-0-9723422-4-7
  ISBN-13: 978-0-9723422-5-4
  ISBN-10: 0-9723422-4-9 (casebound)
  ISBN-10: 0-9723422-5-7 (trade pbk.)
  1. Skis and skiing—Alaska. 2. Skiers—Travel—Alaska. 3. Alaska—Description and travel.
    I. Drake, Stephan, 1976–

GV854.5.A3P69 2005
796.93'09798—dc22
2005019470

stellar

Stellar Books
1209 Pearl Street
Suite 11
Boulder, CO 80302
303-444-4355
www.stellartransmedia.com
www.powderroad.com

Stellar Books is an imprint of Moonlight Publishing.

Moonlight Publishing LLC
2825 Lexington Street
Lafayette, CO 80026 USA
303.641.5675
www.moonlight-publishing.com

CONTENTS

ACKNOWLEDGMENTS

Special thanks to:

Lenir, Urs, SL1, Philip, Amy Rinehart,

Andrew Wilz, Sean Nevin, Matt Ross,

Jon at Pitco, Vivian, Glen, Matt, Josh,

Tucker, Parker, Jon Fossi, Rudy, Roger,

Mike, Adam, Griffin, Mt. Hood Meadows

Ski Patrol, Johann, Bruce and Carrie,

Patrik, Bryan Wolf, Elisa, Chessa and

Jeremy, Amy Howat, Pascal, Miguel,

Fu Kung, Rachel and Landon, Jo Lynn,

Sean Dog, Vasco, Petersburg Jeremy,

Dan, Sverre, Rob, Stian, Trevor, Trask,

JK, and Dean.

THE SEEDS OF POSSIBILITY

Las Leñas is a ski resort nestled in a remote section of the Argentine Andes. It has a phone center—the *telephonica*—which is the only place to make a call to the outside world.

I was hanging out in the *telephonica* on a day marked by low, milky clouds when a familiar face, Alaskan Jesse Tol, walked in. Five years earlier, I had shared a bunk room with him in Las Leñas's employee housing basement—the *subsuelo* or "sub-ghetto" as we used to call it. I hadn't seen him since then.

"What have you been up to, Jesse?"

"Skiing and traveling," he said. There was a lot loaded into that answer, and we acknowledged it with a shared smile.

"What have you been doing?" he now asked me, still holding on to a wide grin.

"Skiing and traveling," I also responded.

Back in the *subsuelo* days of 1997, Jesse had been spending an envious amount of time in helicopters around Valdez, Alaska. He was skiing and shooting photographs and films in a place the media had convinced us was nothing short of skiing's Shangri-La. I think everyone living in that dank, Argentine cave harbored a secret jealousy toward him and his ability to live what seemed like a charmed life in a charmed place.

"Have you been riding a lot of helicopters lately?" I asked.

"Bought a snow machine three years ago and haven't stepped in one since," he proclaimed triumphantly.

My eyes lit up. I was genuinely surprised, "It's a great way to access, eh?"

"The best."

I had been scheming ways to bring a snowmobile to the Andes and was spending quite a lot of time that season scoping the lines and river valleys behind the resort. I told Jesse about my aspirations.

"I was trying to bring my machine down here this year, too," he said. "But shipping is a logistical nightmare, and I didn't get it together in time."

"Can you imagine the potential? The topography here is set up perfectly for sleds," I said, my enthusiasm building. I had found a dreamer who shared my vision, and I felt

comforted to know I wasn't brewing up bizarre ideas in solitude. However, it took only one line for Jesse to redirect my energy.

"Are you kidding? The terrain is set up perfectly in Valdez," he said. "This would be fun, but seriously, it would take me ten days here to get done what I do in an average day in Valdez."

That blew my mind. For some reason I had always thought of Valdez exclusively as a helicopter skiing zone. I hadn't made the connection between him owning a snow-mobile for three years and him having used it in Valdez. My next questions churned through clogged brain gears and burst out in rapid succession. "You can access things easily in Valdez? Can you ski the same terrain as you do with the helis?"

"Are you kidding?" he said. "You can pull off anywhere on Thompson Pass and be skiing in minutes. Sometimes I ride clear up to the helicopter landing zones—right up to the orange landing flags flapping in the wind. The rest of the time it's a twenty-minute hike to the top of lines. Valdez is the best skiing in the world."

"People call me up and say, 'Hey, Jesse, come over here. It's so sick! Come to Europe. Come to some new place in British Columbia.' Everyone is always looking for that next new place. I always go and end up being disappointed."

"I don't come down here to Argentina or go to Europe for the skiing," he continued. "I come for the food, the culture, to meet people, and to experience new things. Sure, there are some great days to be had, but if I really want to go skiing, I just stay in Valdez where I can always find powder. Thompson Pass averages more than 800 inches of snow a year, or something like that."

He then asked me rhetorically, almost teasingly: "Where can you get snow like that with such great access and the best terrain in the world?"

We were on the same powder search. I had skied in a lot of places, but he had skied in even more. His words came from experience, and I trusted them.

"I always thought Valdez and thought helicopters," I continued cautiously, still not quite able to believe. "Is it crowded with sleds?"

"Dude, I can't even find enough people to go with me," Jesse scoffed. "People in Valdez are into football. If you want to watch football, then come to Valdez."

My heart was pounding with some urgency. A new dream was forming. It didn't involve winning the lottery and buying an A-Star, or facing the hassle of shipping a snowmobile to the Andes. It now seemed much simpler: Drive to Valdez from Colorado with a four-stroke snowmobile in tow, and get the most for less. "So you tow your sled up to Thompson Pass?" I asked.

"I usually go right from my house. I leave at 8 AM, come back in at 11 PM, go to sleep, and wake up the next day to do it again. It's the

best combination of terrain and snow in the world, plain and simple."

I finally got around to making my phone call, then ran off into the Argentine night, feeling scattered with the thrill of a new adventure, a new project, a new unknown. I was partially conscious of my foolhardiness in giving credence to everything Jesse had said. But I brushed it aside, knowing that I had never tapped into any real fun without a certain level of naiveté as a prerequisite.

And, as with so many expeditions, the initial idea didn't take more than a few hours to incubate from an exciting conversation into a lingering obsession.

INCEPTION: PEOPLING THE CARAVAN

Despite the enthusiasm of my conversation with Jesse Tol, I passed a full season at the usual resorts, and following the usual crud-by-noon routine. The buzz of a trip up the powder highway to Valdez flickered on chairlift rides and late-night porch conversations, but heavy logistics kept it slotted as a conversation piece.

Over the course of the winter, Swedish photographer Oskar Enander and I tried to put the trip together on a shoestring, but we quickly realized we were doomed by the amount of planning it would take to go. Then that summer came a mysterious moment when passive daydreams were transformed into swirling mind mosquitoes that just wouldn't go away. The notion of this trip to Alaska became a pestering condition that could only be cured by experience. For every day that passed without skiing those lonely powder lines—known only to my imagination—came a guilty sensation that I was missing out on something special.

It had to be done, but this was no solo mission. The trip required time, money, gear, and, most crucially, a tight crew. So I began the hard sell to a group of friends. It could certainly be a photogenic trip, so the first person I approached, a re-recruit, was Oskar Enander.

We had spent the two previous seasons together in Engelberg, Switzerland, shooting ski images for magazines and the ski company I was starting. There had been some amazing days, and we agreed that we could potentially build on our Engelberg work to create a book about the road to Alaska. During the summer we chatted back and forth, but Oskar was in limbo. If we couldn't secure substantial sponsorship for the project, he wouldn't come. The trip would take up two months of his prime shooting season and deal a huge blow to both his wallet and his love life.

In the meantime, I was also talking to Mark Smith, an Oregon native, and long-time ski partner. Mark had been on the Engelberg ski program and also knew Oskar. He happened to be wrapping up a photography project that had kept him in Egypt for a ski season. He was itching to get back on snow, took little convincing, and committed early. The two of us decided to go, regardless of who else wanted to come. We immediately began working to acquire the big-ticket items, including sleds, trucks, and campers.

On a late summer mission, I flew from my home in Colorado to Oregon to pick up a used truck and a circa 1970's Alaskan Camper.

On that short trip to the Northwest, I stayed at Gavin Cummings's house in Portland. Gavin, Mark, and I were all friends from Las Leñas. One night, with the city sleeping and a couple glasses of Fernet Branca in hand, I pitched Gavin the merits of four-stroke snowmobiles, a new style of access, and all the empty mountain ranges on the way to Alaska. He listened and entertained the idea but didn't commit because he had just earned a new position as an avalanche forecaster at Mt. Hood Meadows.

By mid-fall, Mark had a Yamaha four-stroke in his possession, and I had a sled on order. Oskar was, at this point, not coming. He couldn't manage the expense and the time it would take to fly over from Europe and buy a snowmobile. Then, I happened to send him an issue of *Powder* magazine that contained one of his photographs. By pure coincidence, that issue also featured an article on snowmobile-assisted skiing in Canada. A week later, I got a surprise phone call from Europe.

"Dude, I am coming on this trip," Oskar announced. "I don't care anymore if we don't have enough money. I saw that issue of *Powder*, and the photos were amazing. I am doing this."

Mark, Oskar, and I were in. Gavin was on the fringe, but it took nothing more than a wild turn of the weather to bring him into the fold. He explains it this way:

With an Indian summer that wouldn't stop and every offshore storm hitting well to the north or south, the season in the Northwest

wasn't shaping up into anything special. By late December the mountain still hadn't opened, and the lack of work was taking a toll on my bank account. I'd been hired as one of the avalanche fore-casters, and I didn't want to jeop-ardize my new position, but the idea of skiing uncharted terrain in British Columbia and Alaska, not to mention high adventure on the open road, was calling me. All the elements were coming together: Stephan and Mark had already bought their snowmobiles, Oskar was committed to the point of abandoning a season of shooting in Engelberg, and the only missing element was someone to film the whole experience. I'd seen my fair share of movies, knew what I liked, and figured it couldn't be that hard. Four-thousand dollars worth of shooting and editing equipment later, I guess I was in.

In late-January, Mark and I were in Las Vegas at the annual ski industry tradeshow trying to hustle some extra equipment for the trip when Gavin picked up a one-way ticket from Portland to meet us. The three of us then drove back to Colorado to prep for the journey north. Oskar would fly over from Switzerland two weeks later.

03

ENDLESS GEAR

The trip, in many ways, quickly became a struggle with gear. If one were to plan an adventure like this with a solid truck and snowmobile in their possession, it would be fairly easy to round up some miscellaneous gear and hit the road. We were in a different predicament altogether. All we had was an idea and our skis. There was an arsenal of equipment to acquire, and with our meager budget, we were forced to cut corners on many big-ticket purchases. It wasn't long before we were living by the adage: You get what you pay for.

The one item we didn't skimp on was snowmobiles. Using snowmobiles for ski access is not a new concept, but our crew had been reluctant to embrace sleds prior to recent advancements in four-stroke engines. The two-stroke engines of snowmobiling's past were, in our eyes, heavy polluters. Four-strokes reduce emissions considerably, making the snowmobile a more environmentally conscionable tool.

However, four-strokes in themselves don't present a case-closed argument in favor of snowmobile use for ski access,

and the complex and polarizing conversation surrounding snowmobile ethics could occupy the length of this book. We continue to straddle both sides of the debate. On one hand, we have a passion for wilderness and non-motorized spaces, and on the other, a passion for skiing and access in wild terrain. The obvious contradiction leaves us in a lonely community of sled skiers. For this trip, the advent of cleaner engines on mountain-worthy sleds was enough to push us in favor of using Yamaha four-strokes. Without the sleds, we could have visited only a tiny fraction of the terrain we covered.

Although our sleds were shiny and new at the outset, our trucks were old and tired. We rounded up two 1993 diesel, three-quarter-ton trucks with high mileage. The white Chevrolet quickly became known as "Great White," and the red Ford earned the creative moniker "The Red Truck." We loved them both like family, but each one would succumb to a sizable number of frustrating mechanical issues over the course of our travels.

The trouble started in mid-January when, after buying The Red Truck in partnership with a friend, Mark left Portland, Oregon to come to Colorado to train for a month. Just sixty miles outside of Portland, on an icy bridge, another truck lost control in front of him. He T-boned it and arrived in Colorado with The Red Truck's mangled grill and headlights barely attached with duct tape and bungee cords. The Red Truck's injury yielded extensive damage, and ultimately a salvage title. Meanwhile, in the early stages of my preparation, Great White endured glow plug

and transfer case surgery. And so began the acquisition of more frequent flyer miles than we ever hoped for—via our credit cards.

The third integral item on our gear list was the truck campers. We opted for circa-1970s Alaskan Campers that rise for camping and sink hydraulically to a lower profile for more efficient driving. They would be our home for three months. They were great machines, but their condition when we bought them (the camper on Great White was $400), made for a lot of prep work. After all our upgrades and mini hop-up projects, we could have easily purchased newer models for a better deal.

In addition, nothing was easy on the repair circuit. I bought a propane heater for Great White called "Mr. Big Buddy." A week after the purchase, Mr. Big Buddy was placed on safety recall. After a number of phone calls to the Mr. Big Buddy people, I learned that the unit couldn't be replaced until a verdict on their national recall plan came from the government. We were forced to take our defective Mr. Big Buddy along with us, which started a string of nervous explosion jokes. To his credit, defective Mr. Big Buddy worked sans nocturnal explosions. We eventually picked up a replacement model at the U.S. Post Office in Haines, Alaska.

The months of January and February were spent at the hardware store and with auto mechanic. We modified brackets, built ski holders, installed and wired solenoid switches, stopped leaks, copied keys, and purchased and put in place propane tanks, gear sleds, dishes, cutlery, mini speakers, and

insulation. We mounted eight pairs of skis with bindings, installed Vibram soles on ski boots, put studs on tires, twice repaired 4x4 transfer case switches, bought and modified roof racks, sorted gear from Mammut, loaded iPods with music, found and purchased heavy-duty Sorels and boat ladders via the Internet, broke and replaced trailer couplers and loading ramps, installed camper interior fans, wired camper batteries, ordered and subsequently attached snowmobile ski racks, rigged new wiring on trailers, re-jetted the snowmobiles, and changed the oil on everything.

When Oskar arrived, we had already been working on our preparations for weeks. The four of us spent a week together in Boulder trolling the aisles of McGuckin's hardware for miscellaneous parts. We then eventually migrated to Aspen, where we went to train and repair more things. Long days blended skinning for fitness, sled rides, vertical at the resort, and ever-present afternoons at the hardware store. Even though we hadn't yet begun our travels, we were scoring some good powder and honing what would become perhaps our most vital newly-learned skill: how to dig out a stuck snowmobile.

Mark's Camper
+ Build Couch / BED
+ Propane Tank
+ SPEAKERS for Ipod sewel
+ HOME RUDY CAMPER
+ BOX

Mark's BODY
+ Chiro / ASPENCLUB

MARK'S BOOTS
+ VIBRAM
+ TAI SKIE

MARK'S SKIS
+ TABLAS

MARK'S TRAILER
+ ORDER RAMP
+ Extra PINS

MARK SLED
+ 6 SPARK PLUGS

Stefan's Camper
+ Lower + Mount
+ TRIM FRONT
+ PROPANE + REGULATOR
+ DRIVER BIG BUDDY
+ Selunoid switch
+ INverter for music
+ Mount Roof Box — ADHESIVE?
+ CLOTHES LINES
+ SPEAKERS
+ BACKGAMMON Board
+ Mount Propane Tank
+ Storage

STEPHAN'S BOOTS
+ MOLD LINERS @ Larry's
+ NEW SPOILERS
+ EPOXY

Pizza - Gosatutchy Beer for ANDREW for Tunes

TRAILER
+ New Hitch Thing
+ Install Jack
+ Licconee Plate
+ wiring

VICTOR
+ SKID PLATE

04

DEPARTURE: THE TRUCKS MOVE

It was ten days after our planned departure date, and we were still in Colorado trying to transform our trucks and campers into machines worthy of the long road ahead. Constant trips to the hardware store and mechanic were stretching into infinity, and despite a couple of good sunset sessions on Independence Pass, Mark reasoned that we could spend the next three months perfecting our trucks and never leave. The pressure of not being one mile closer to Alaska was mounting.

On a Friday, we finally pulled the plug on our old bath water of repairs and decided to start the journey. However, at 10 PM I was still prepping Great White's propane system while Oskar packed our gear and clothes into the truck's tight quarters. The temperature was dropping, and it had started to snow. We took a break and went inside to eat the farewell feast my mother had cooked us. With full stomachs, we walked back to the trucks. A policeman came by the Red Truck and asked

Mark and Gavin if they were leaving that evening. The camper's running lights and the rumble of idling diesel had begun to draw complaints from the neighborhood. Mark and Gavin hooked up their snowmobiles and disappeared into the storm.

We continued packing Great White, but it wasn't until 2 AM that Oskar and I, completely exhausted, fired up the engine and let a Peter Tosh album twang through the truck's shoddy speakers. We crawled through the streets of Aspen and the fast-falling snowflakes of promise that were accumulating on Highway 82. We were in the dreamy womb of a large storm, and as a skier, you couldn't ask for a better start to a trip.

To add to the omen, an enormous old buck appeared on the side of the road. He stood motionless with his large hooves balanced on the road's white line. His eyes peered straight into the cab of our truck. As we drove slowly by, he told us we were on our way. We were leaving behind the glue of everyday life and reentering a space with the possibility of greeting transcendence with one sweet turn.

Great White and the red truck made it only forty miles beyond Aspen that first night. We pulled into Glenwood Springs and fell asleep in the Wal-Mart parking lot.

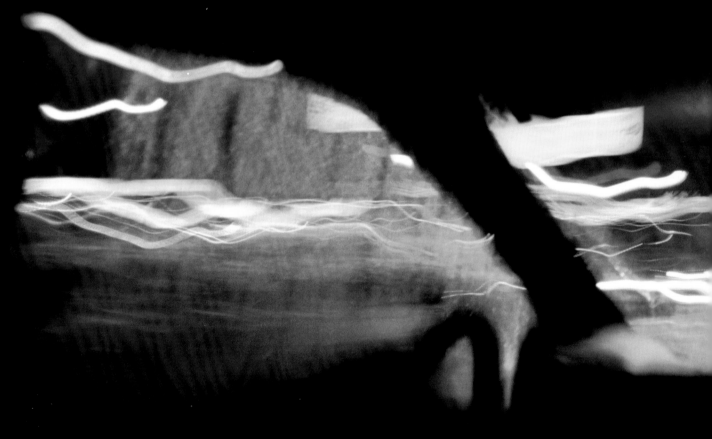

05

JACKSON

On our route northwest, the first major stop was Jackson, Wyoming. We met an old friend and experienced sled skier, Glen Wade, and began to taste the great generosity that became typical along the road north. While he and his friends graciously showed us around the backcountry for a few days, I stole away here and there to participate in a magazine ski test at nearby Teton Village.

Ski culture can be a fine contrast between Apollonian and Dionysian impulses, and during one night of our stay, both elements came into play. I had to be up early the next morning, and spent a peaceful night alone in the camper repairing the Vibram soles on my boots by candlelight. Meanwhile, at the other end of town, the party was in high gear. Mark describes the action in his journal on the following pages.

Last night I watched Oskar turn into a Viking. The metamorphosis started at the Powder Week dinner. He was taking advantage of free drinks, and by the time we made it to the Shady Lady (boats could easily be named after bars), Oskar was lit. I didn't stay very long, but I guess his dance performances have become legend.

The next morning, I arrived at Glen's apartment. I found Gavin and asked him if he wanted to get some breakfast. He smiled and said, "Do you want some eggs?" I followed his eyes and saw that Oskar had attempted the impossible: He had tried to cook a twelve egg omelette in an English Muffin-sized skillet. The kitchen was a disaster. Egg shells littered the floor and the stovetop looked like a compost pile. I thought, "Christ, Oskar, we just met these people." I walked into the living room and found Oskar in a fetal position on the couch. He wore a pained expression as if he'd just been kicked in the crotch. Egg vomit was everywhere.

I heard someone descend the stairs, and felt uneasy because I knew there was some explaining to do. It was Matt, but before I could say anything, he laughed and yelled upstairs, "THE SCANDINAVIAN HURLED ALL OVER OUR LIVING ROOM!" That made me smile. I like it when people can laugh at the messes we bring into each other's lives. Gavin and I cleaned the place up and then helped Oskar out of the apartment and into the truck.

I drove to Teton Village with Oskar. He was curled up in the passenger seat like a sunburnt snail. I found the crowded parking lot reserved for the Powder

Week Ski test, and met up with Stephan who was waiting to help move Oskar to Great white. Oskar groaned painfully in Swedish as we hoisted him into the camper, and after giving him water, it looked like a merciful sleep would take him to a better place.

Stephan told me he had to get back to the ski test and handed me a free pass. As I was getting ready to make use of it, the camper door opened and Oskar reemerged. He was standing on the tailgate, struggling to keep his balance, and then it happened: He started spewing stomach bile onto the pavement. It sounded like suffering, and his mouth looked like a faucet that wouldn't turn off. Ski industry people, vacationers and their children, they all stopped and stared as if they were at a zoo. Aware that he had an audience, Oskar wiped his mouth and yelled, "THIS IS NORMAL! THIS ALWAYS HAPPENS! THIS IS NORMAL!" I couldn't keep from laughing. I felt the need to translate, to tell all the puzzled onlookers that Oskar meant he can never keep water down after a 10 hour bender. But I just stood there, embarrassed and laughing, and watched all those stunned faces trying to comprehend why Oskar vomits from tailgates everyday.

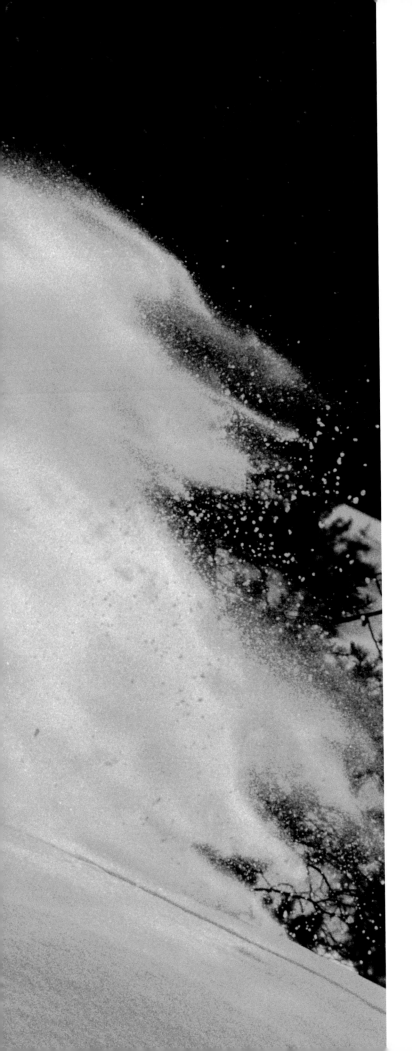

06

PORTLAND

Coming from Jackson, we arrived in Gavin's hometown of
Portland, where we stayed for a few days before crossing the
border into Canada. Mark and I stayed down in the city
attending to last minute business, while Gavin and Oskar
made daily trips up to Mt. Hood to shoot photos. Gavin tells
the story as follows:

*Except for a couple of nights in a backcountry cabin in Hyder
and countless nights in the camper, Portland proved to be the
last roof over our heads for months and, for Stephan and me,
the last shower for weeks.*

*The weather in Oregon was still unseasonably warm when we
arrived. Mt. Hood Meadows had been opening, closing, and
reopening again, with ribbons of snow weaving from the top
lift station to the base. We didn't expect any epic skiing there,
but with high pressure and temperatures in the 60s, a backcountry kicker session was in order, and Mt. Hood was a great
place for it.*

The mountain forms a commanding presence on the Cascade skyline. It's a lone volcano that gets healthy evening alpenglow that slowly builds, lingers, and then crescendoes to a vibrant rose. The light was just what Oskar was looking for to round out his images. My days of going big in the quarterpipe were dwindling, so I invited my brother Griffin to come along. Having been at the forefront of the progressive freestyle movement in the Northwest for years, he was the person to deliver the kind of shot Oskar was looking for.

During our two days of shooting, Oskar and I leisurely made our way up to the mountain from Portland. We picked up Griffin at Windell's along the way, took our time, and let the day mature and the snow soften. By 4 PM,

the upper part of the resort was closed, so we'd make our way to the southwest boundary where the light stays the longest.

The first day, we built our quarterpipe-shaped kicker. It had a little too much compression on the takeoff and would rocket you straight up and then back down onto the lip. On the second day, we deepened the in-run and rounded out the transition. With a light Chinook wind and thin stratus clouds smoldering on the horizon, the scene was finally set. Griffin and I hit it long after it became too dark to see the in-run, but it didn't matter. We were having fun. Building, shaping, and hitting the quarterpipe with my brother was the last bit of good familiarity I needed for the journey ahead.

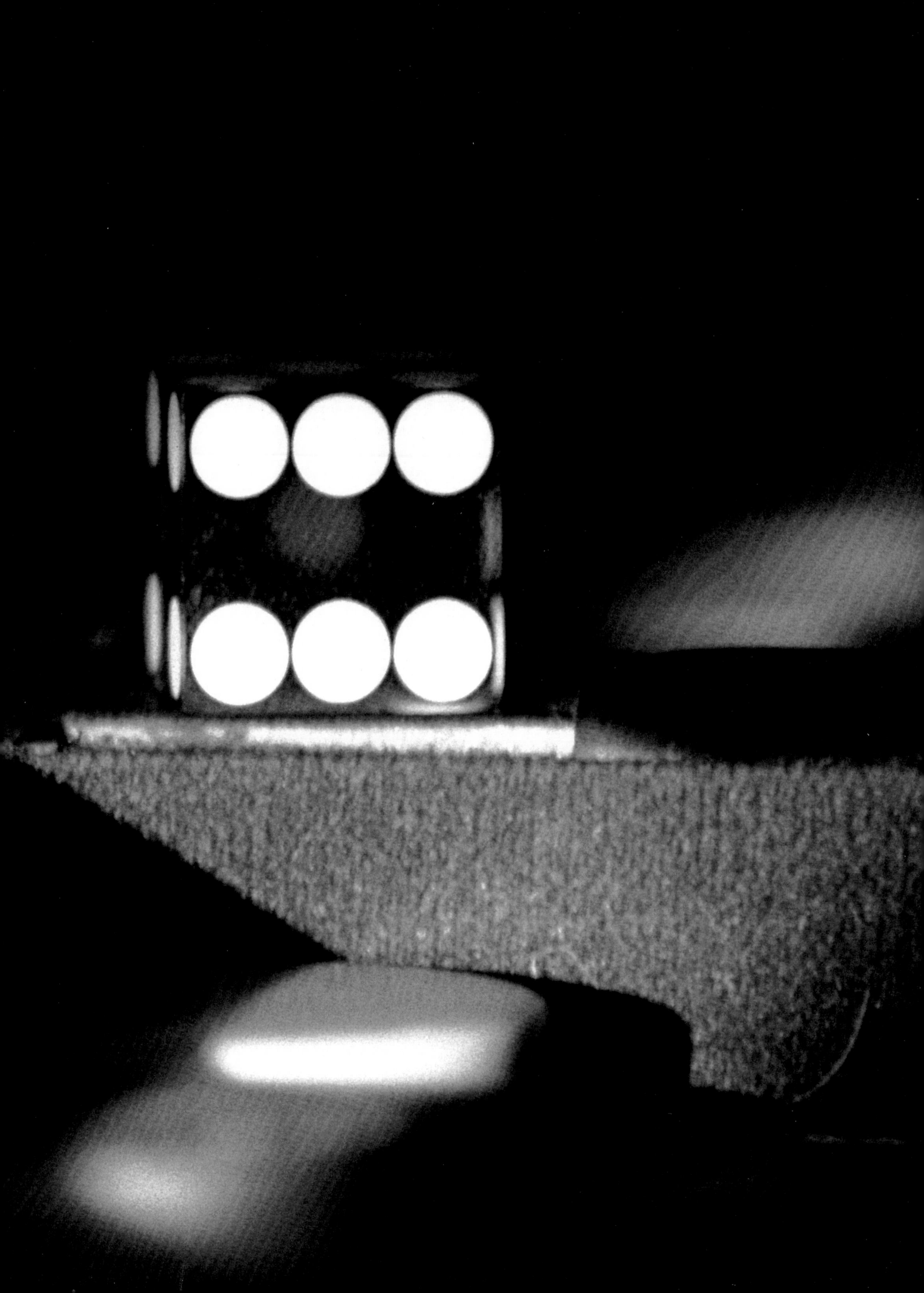

07

HOPE, BRITISH COLUMBIA

After crossing the Canadian border, we passed into the landscape that had toyed with my curiosity since a childhood of reading ski magazines. My fingertips had traced British Columbia's lines on the globe countless times, and I had wasted long hours on the Internet finding pictures of its remote towns and researching the snowfall statistics for its different zones.

Now, as the road signs changed from miles to kilometers, I savored the feeling of actually realizing my dreams. It was like showing up at the Aguille du Midi on a big day for the first time or watching waves crash onto Hawaii's North Shore—the sensation of finally experiencing a place popular culture has transformed into myth. Valdez, Alaska, would elicit a similar sensation a month later.

Despite this excitement, southern British Columbia, at first impression, didn't differ too much from the American Northwest in terms of architecture or road vistas. We drove in the rain past familiar-looking stretches of trailers, farmhouses, and billboards adorned with the same global brands. Not far over the border, we stopped to have Great

White's wiper motor fixed in a town named Hope. The mechanic at the GM dealer asked me with an honest smile if I wanted to "give'er" on the repairs. It was not until the delivery of that phrase that cultural difference breathed, and I began to pick up on the warm and unfamiliar friendliness that runs through Canada.

We sat in a coffee shop in Hope while the mechanic worked on Great White. Our cell phones were now out of range, so we used a pay phone in the rainy street to call the province's heli operators for snow reports. Much like the American Northwest, the normally snowy latitudes of southern British Columbia were all at low tide. We were bummed that we would have to pass up some classic terrain, but also encouraged by rumors trickling in of a big winter up north.

Sensing that the clock was ticking on our adventure—and knowing that every day on snow is precious—we re-boarded our trucks at dusk, turned the new wipers to high, and joined a parade of massive logging trucks in a strong, two-day push north through British Columbia. Having long wondered about the stretch of land we were traveling through, I found rolling hills, dense pines, logging operations, and winter pastures—not the spired, snowy peaks of my dreams.

At each gas station and coffee shop we would learn again that this was a lean year, but that farther up the road, the mountains were rife with snow. The suspense continued to grow as Oskar became antsy for photos, and we all wanted to ski again.

We finally rolled into the northern town of Terrace under a hard rain, but the clouds would occasionally lift high enough for us to see steep mountains covered in a deep snowpack.

The push from Oregon ended up lasting three days and included twelve hundred miles, fourteen PB&J's, two detours, hundreds of dollars in diesel, and no showers.

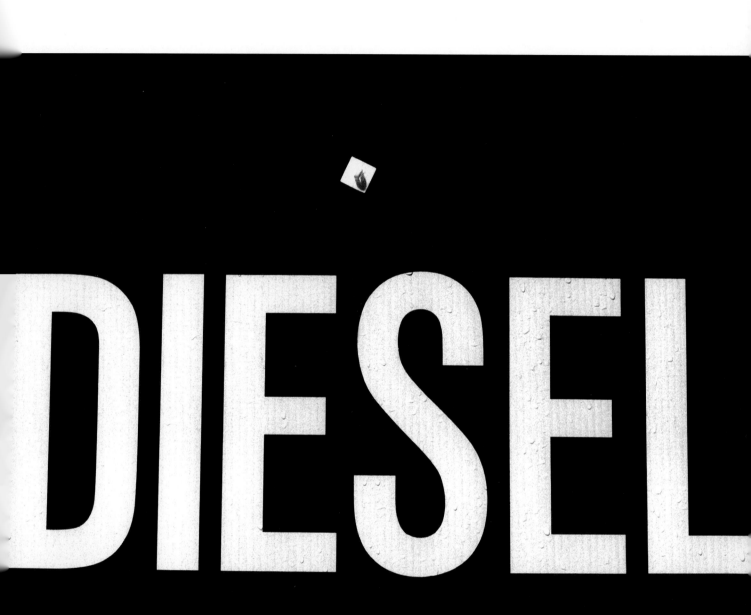

08

SLAM, OUR BALL, FOUND

In the most canonical of ski films, *The Blizzard of Aahhhs*, the protagonists travel to the Chamonix valley. In a smoky bar, they meet a Kiwi named Murray Ball who guides them through the mountains during their stay.

In a similar manner, throughout our travels we relied on generous local knowledge to get us to the right places. Armed with only our lackluster snowmobile skills, we were in need of our own Murray Ball as we entered the wild mountains of northern Canada. Following a long list of names, and not long after failing to cross paths with one Mackenzie Funk, we were gifted the phone number of Mr. Johann Slam. The word was that Johann protected the road to the coast from avalanches and regularly used his sled for snowboard access.

Following the tip, we drove through a fog- and rain-drenched night on a fine stretch of wilderness road to reach his town. Our trucks pulled in after midnight and found deserted streets lined with large, otherworldly snow banks. After a drink and a round of pool to decompress from the road, we parked the rigs for the night behind a bar dubbed the Pink Palace.

We woke the next morning to raindrops piercing slushy puddles. The clouds and fog were hanging so low that they obscured the rooftops of what, in daylight, could now be seen as a recessed mining town nestled into a beautiful fjord. Despite the bad weather, we had breakfast, found another pay phone, and contacted Slam. With only a reference from a friend of his, Johann agreed to rendezvous on Main Street and take us on a "snort," or sled ride, to check out the terrain.

We geared up for skiing for the first time in a week and drove to meet Johann in the drizzling rain. Drawing closer to his truck, we saw a man who appeared different from anything I expected. He could have just stepped off a fishing boat after a long stint on a cold ocean. His burly, thick frame was clothed in bright-yellow slicker pants, orange XTRATUF boots, and a black hooded sweatshirt.

As I opened the door of the truck to meet him, I could make out a wiry, dark beard littered across the bottom of his broad face and wild hair flowing out of a tattered wool hat. His bright eyes smiled with an ageless fire that obscured whether he was thirty or fifty years old. Before Johann Slam ever opened his mouth, we knew we had found our man.

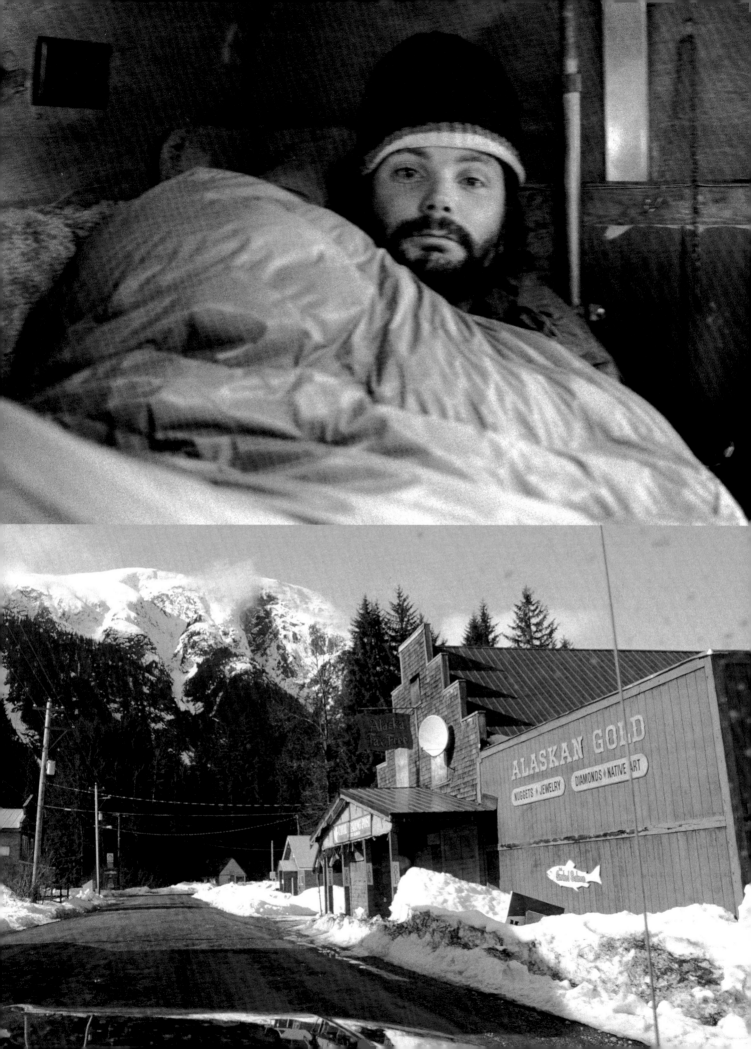

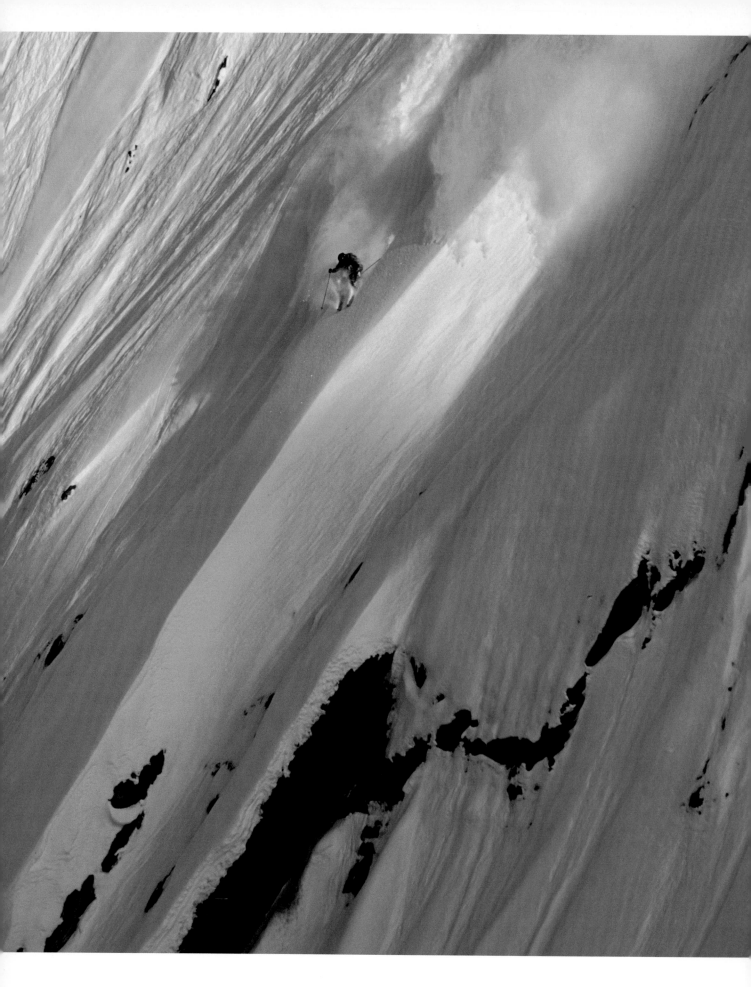

09

MURPHY'S

The use of snowmobiles as access tools was an uncertain experiment. Before the trip, we had only used sleds on groomed cat roads, and we quickly found that in the deep snow and big mountains of the North, the sleds became difficult machines to manage. As Mark put it, we underwent baptism by fire.

We became progressively more efficient as the trip went on, but the amount of time we spent digging, yanking, and struggling with our sleds bordered on the absurd. With two twelve-year-old trucks, campers from the 1970s, and neophyte sledding skills, we were bound to have things go wrong. On one three-day stretch in British Columbia, almost everything did.

The four of us were shooting the breeze at the trailhead before our first outing with Johann Slam when the conversation was interrupted by ugly, guttural sounds from the corner of the parking lot. Johann stopped mid-sentence, and we all looked over to see Victor, as my snowmobile had come to be called, shaking in a spastic dance. The sled then convulsed even more violently, backfired twice, and died. Silence settled over us, apart from the low hiss of steam and boiling coolant seeping from the hood.

Victor had been tuned to run in the lean, high elevations of Colorado and wasn't taking well to the oxygen-rich sea-level air. He needed professional help, and the nearest shop was four hours away in the wrong direction. I got in Great White and drove four hours back to Terrace, camped in the mechanic's parking lot, spent a few hundred more Canadian dollars, and then drove back to Hyder the next day, which happened to be my birthday.

Exhausted and demoralized, I pulled in during the early evening and met up with Mark, who had been waiting for me all day and looked equally spent. The rest of the crew had gone forty kilometers up to the hut where we would be staying for a few days. He stayed behind to show me the way. It was too late in the day for us to move to a higher elevation, so instead, we stopped at the Glacier Inn and managed to get Hyderized (a Friday-night rite of passage involving a shot of grain alcohol and fire) even though it was Saturday.

We then parked the trucks on a pier by the ocean. Under a bright, starry sky, we ran some gypsy music through the camper's stereo, played backgammon, and talked the blues about how zapped we were and how hard it had been to get in a decent day of skiing. Those few hours of quiet downtime by the ocean saved what was an otherwise rough way to spend a birthday.

We woke up the next morning filled with positive energy and ready to make our move into the mountains to meet Oskar and Gavin. Our enthusiasm didn't last long. The access road to the trailhead featured foot-and-half-deep ice ruts which kept the truck crawling at five miles per hour and broke the lights on our trailer. We finally decided to stop driving and push on with our sleds. Once out of the truck, I ripped my jacket in half on a piece of metal sticking out of the camper. Then, on the sled ride up the access road, I managed to re-paralyze Victor by overheating a set of plastic runners—effectively gluing them to the snowmobile's rubber track. Victor was down for another hour while we figured that one out. The trip took three hours more than it should have, and by the time we got to the hut, Mark and I were in no mood to answer any questions.

During our first ski outing, the four of us found it impossible to climb the key hill that served as the gateway to the best terrain in the area. For an entire afternoon, we

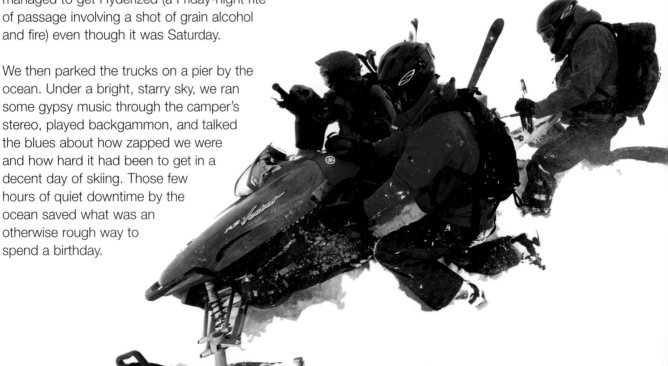

climbed, got stuck, dug ourselves out, and repeated. At one point, two local slednecks, who had already climbed the hill a number of times, stopped to ask if we were planning on camping there that night.

The next morning, we finally managed the hill, but not before Mark got bucked off his sled within ten minutes of leaving the hut. His sled rag-dolled down the hill he was trying to climb and wound up broken at the bottom. Johann jokingly told us that each time your sled pulls a full rotation while flipping, it costs you $100, and in this case, which included bent handlebars and a damaged throttle, Johann was right.

Only a few hours later, I was finally on my skis and jumping a cornice when I blew the landing, and broke my hand. The injury would later be misdiagnosed by the Russian doctor in town, and lead to the to permanent disfigurement of my knuckles.

We tried to escape the hut the next morning under light snowfall. My hand was non-functioning, and I was forced to operate my sled's throttle with my elbow. Mark, on the other hand, was forced to drive his sled at maximum speed to keep his damaged throttle running. He was darting around like a maniac on the edge, while I gimped along at a snail's pace, grimacing in pain.

I was making slow progress with my elbow when I came over the crest of a steep downhill and saw Oskar standing at the bottom—without his snowmobile or the 150-pound gear sledge he had been towing. Gavin pulled up next to me. We looked closer and noticed both the snowmobile and sledge wedged into a deep creek bed, one hundred feet below Oskar. Gavin and I exchanged a glance as if to say, "When is this going to end?"

The situation looked utterly hopeless. We had a thousand pounds of machinery augered vertically into a frozen riverbed that was flanked by steep, eight-foot walls. But after two hours of digging, and some creative snow engineering, Gavin, Oskar, and Mark got the sled out by building a massive ramp.

Shortly after that, Oskar, who had been a stellar navigator during our Jackson epic, led us down the wrong drainage. At the same time, his sled sprung an oil leak that required attention.

When we arrived at the truck, hours later, Oskar opened the door to the camper and looked over at me with a flustered expression. "What the hell did you do in here?" he asked.

"What do you mean?" I said.

"Look!"

I walked over and looked inside. There were piles of runny shit all over the floor and cushions. "It looks like an animal crawled in through the window while we were gone," I observed. The night before, there had been a pine martin near the hut. Oskar hadn't liked the looks of the animal, and he had called it a mink.

Now, looking utterly disgusted, he proclaimed, "It was the damn mink! A mink shat in our house."

All we could do, at that point, was laugh.

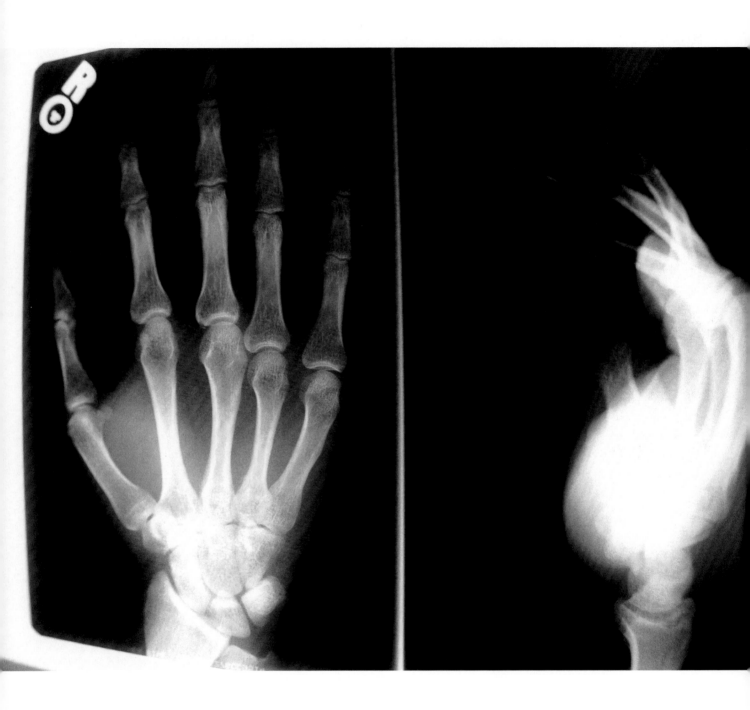

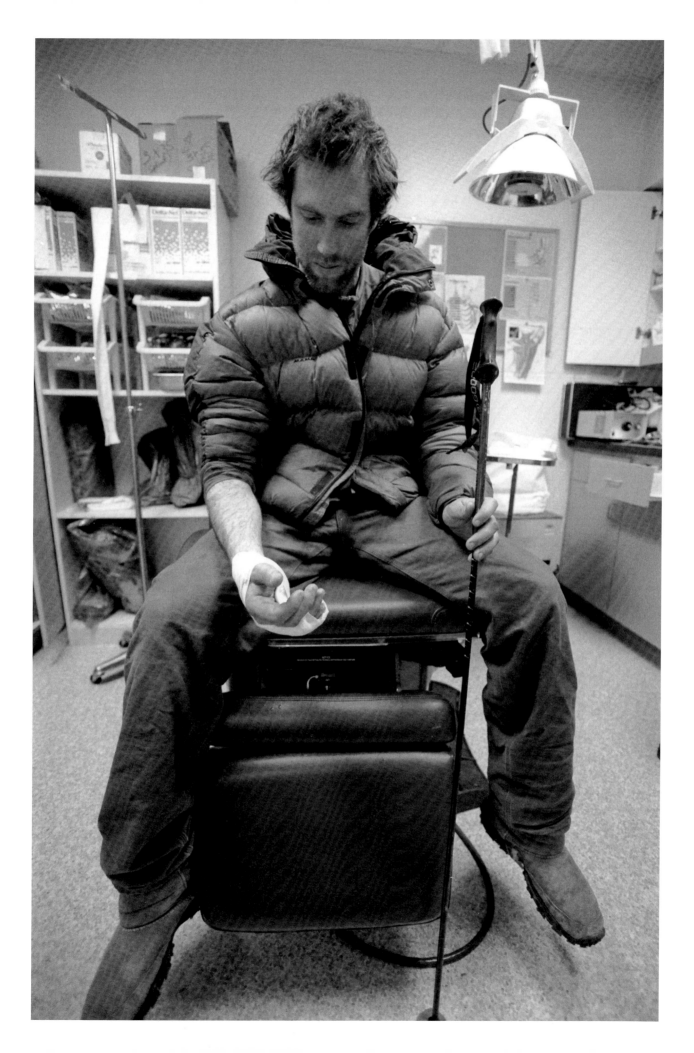

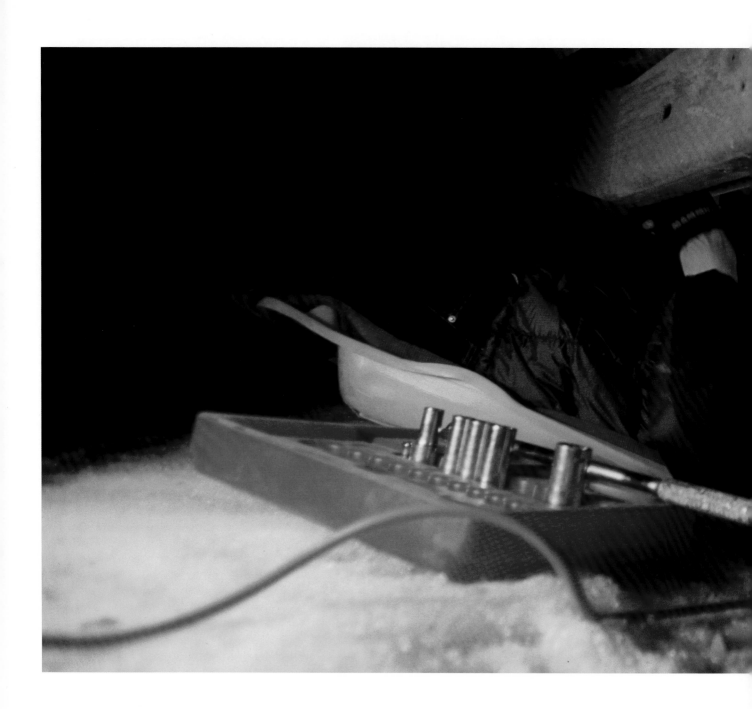

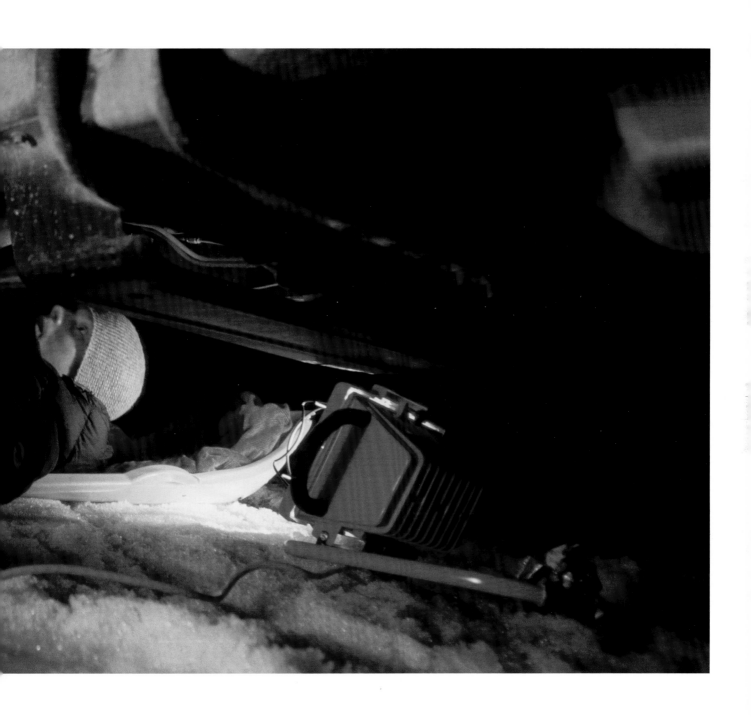

10

THE FREEZER

Johann Slam led us up the Cassiar Highway on a journey through long expanses of winter road so desolate that we often had time to pull the trucks side-by-side, have a chat, and not worry about other vehicles. Our destination was an abandoned mining town that had been closed for a decade. We arrived to discover a postmodern relic of gnarled buildings, churches, and trucks. The only functioning infrastructure left was a lone telephone booth surrounded by hundreds of miles of wilderness peaks.

Despite the disaster in Hyder, our theory of self-sufficient ski travel in wild country was holding up—albeit barely. In the area's open terrain, Johann was quick to show us what was possible on a snowmobile. We were soon dropping ourselves close to the top of remote ridges, and to the delight of our battered egos, we didn't get stuck or break gear.

In the end, the weather would sabotage our skiing efforts. On the second day, the temperature dove as thick clouds moved into the zone. It got cold, and then it got even colder. Finally, the

thermometer dropped yet another notch and sent us into a mind-numbing freeze. With the propane furnace on The Red Truck conveniently broken and Mr. Big Buddy only allowed to fire during daylight for fear of catastrophic explosion at night, I woke one morning to find the camper's thermometer hovering at negative twenty degrees. Life slowed to a painful crawl. Aided by my freshly broken hand, it took me hours to complete basic chores like eating, gearing up, and dropping a deuce.

The clouds and cold lingered, and to pass the downtime, we began exploring the mine's surreally twisted pieces of iron, sheet metal, and pastel-painted structures. It was not long before we discovered that we could spin ski laps on the mini mountain of asbestos tailings that rose from the ruins. Ironically, the tailing run would become the greatest source of vertical while in town.

A day came when the skies cleared enough for us to push deep into the surrounding range. The cold would not release its cruel grip though, and Oskar's feet froze halfway through the morning. Despite everyone's best attempts at a field massage to get the blood moving, he was forced to return to camp. Oskar eventually made a full recovery and escaped unscathed. Mark, however, wasn't as lucky. He stayed out, and over the course of the day, developed frostbite on his toes.

The clouds rolled back in that evening, and we retreated inside Great White and to the relative warmth of Mr. Big Buddy. It was a good time to indulge in backgammon, a large pot of pasta, and the stories, politics, and laughter of Johann Slam.

The temperature never warmed and Johann finally had to drive back home to work. Our group bid him farewell as a light snow fell from low clouds. We waited one more night for the weather to clear, but the next morning came colder and grayer still. We left the telephone booth and continued northward.

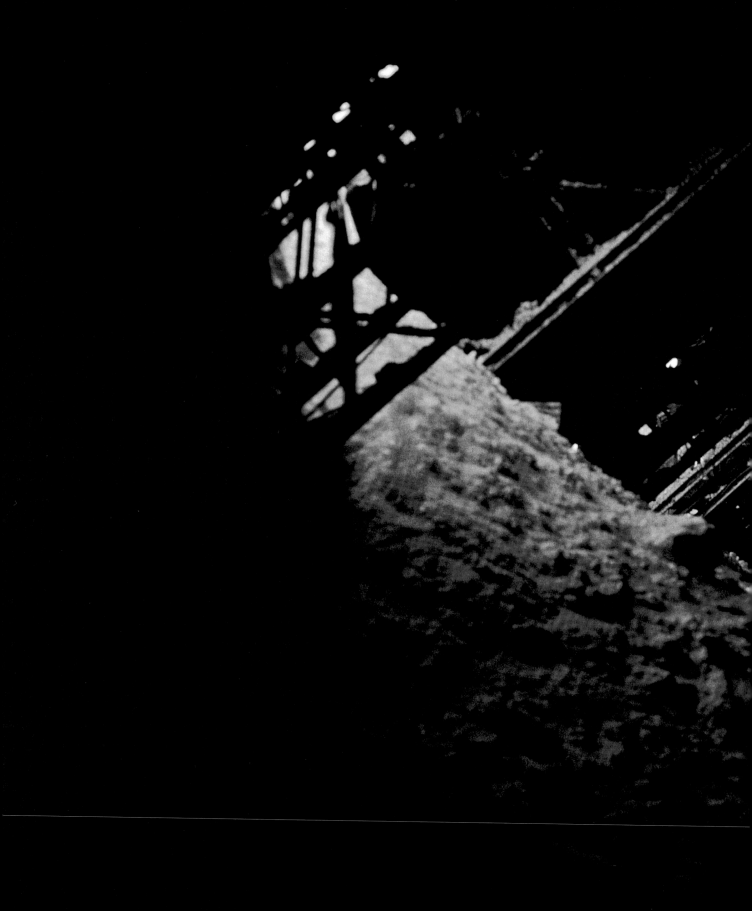

We're in Cassiar now. It's a desolate landscape of stark contrasts; awe-inspiring mountains spike the western horizon, yet we're surrounded by an industrial ghost town of steel structures and asbestos tailings.

Last night, on the drive in, this place looked different. We were a mile from our campsite when the sky began to change. The horizon lit up with an emerald brilliance that danced in my eyes like an emotion. It took me a couple seconds to understand what was happening because I had never seen the Northern Lights before. I don't remember when I first saw the Pacific ocean or an autumn sunset, but I think I know the sense of wonder I must have felt.

Johann told us there's a Northern Lights center in Whitehorse. It caters to Asian tourists who consider the Aurora Borealis a source of fertility. They watch the lights and then go inside and get after it for as long as they can — at least I think that's what it's all about. I wish I was having that kind of fun right now because everything is frozen here and a milky sky has us camper-bound. We just need high pressure and something to get scared on and everything will be good.

We just passed a sign that welcomed us into the Yukon. Gavin is at the wheel and Nick Drake is singing about a place to be. It's stormy outside. Snow is snaking across the road and the wind is pushing hard at our nose. This part of the Alcan Highway is hypnotizing. It's lined with skinny pine trees whose naked trunks move like the frames from an old animated film.

We left Cassiar this morning. We're now calling it the freezer because it was exactly that. The terrain was amazing, and the sled travel was easy because we were following frozen river systems. We found some magical cirques, and unlike Stewart, we didn't have any mechanical or rider induced epics. We're no longer upside-down-and-shoveling like we were in January. Sleds can be humbling but the struggle to get better has been worth it. Some of the descents we did in Cassiar could only have happened with a heli. Couloirs that would take a couple days to reach with touring gear are happening for us in less than an hour. But Gavin still thinks the sleds are a wild card. He's right. There's always some sort of agro waiting to slow you down, but the reliability of our legs could never get us to the places we want to go.

Tonight we'll be in White Horse. I need to wash my sleeping bag and I need to wash me because we smell the same. I think I tagged my toes pretty good. They've swollen to a familiar color of blue, but it's worse than I've ever felt it before. I didn't listen to my body and it's screaming at me now.

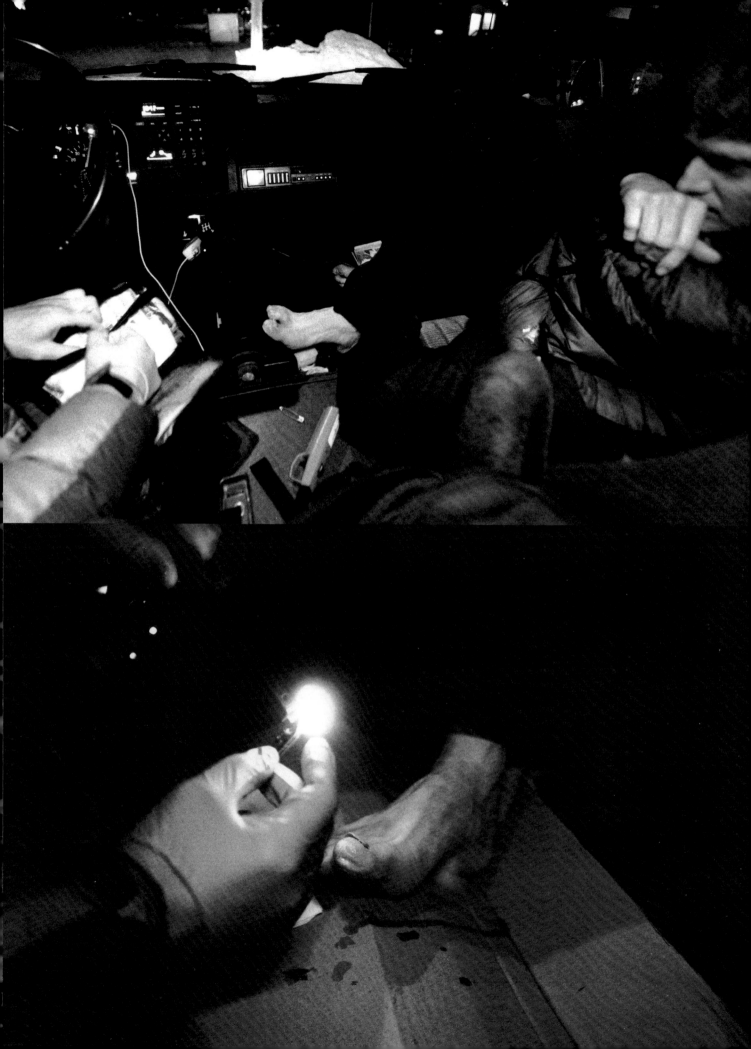

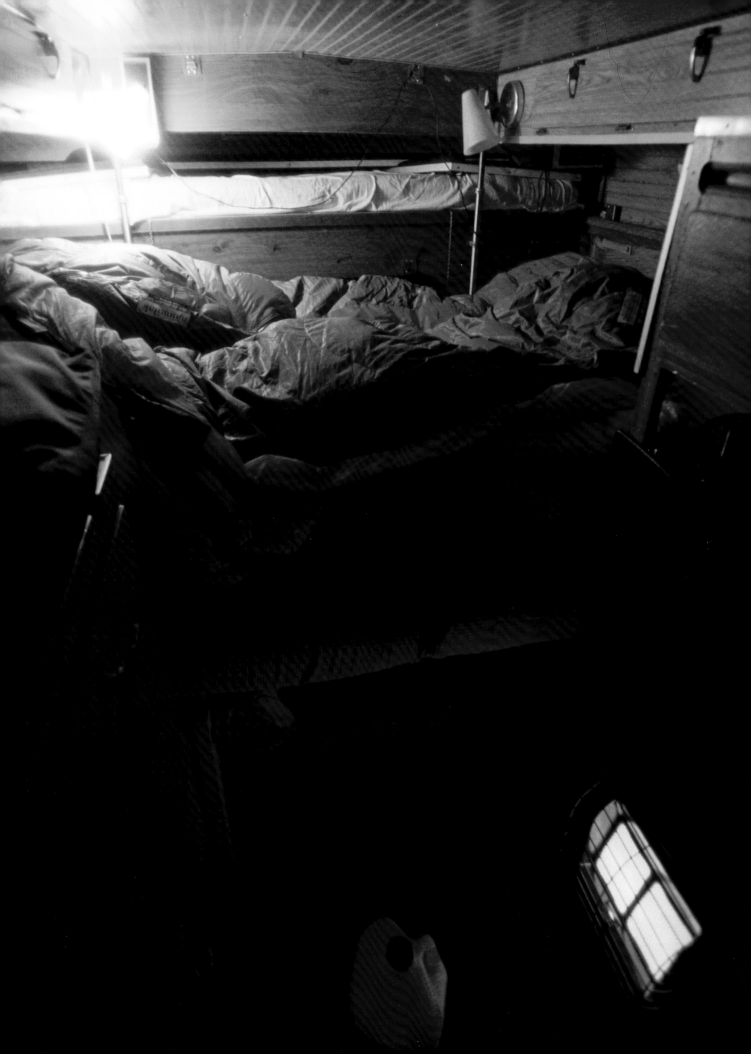

11

IT WAS A WEDNESDAY

After parting with Slam, we pointed the trucks north toward the economic and cultural capital of the Yukon, Whitehorse. We arrived to find what was by no means a large town, but a good place to lick our wounds while waiting for repairs on our abused sleds. Mark's frostbitten blisters were popped in a ceremonial truck ritual, and we managed our first shower in three weeks at the local hot springs. Despite some comforts, Whitehorse sits on the interior and isn't exactly warm in March. With expectations of a warmer climate and deep snow, we were all anxious to push on to Haines. Oskar and I hit the road, while Mark and Gavin stayed behind one extra night to wait for the delivery of a sled part.

When we rolled over Haines Pass and back into Alaska, it was a Tuesday night. Snow was falling harder and faster than any place we had been since leaving Aspen. Great White was churning through the deep snow in four-wheel drive, the temperatures were reasonable, and life seemed good again. We chose a campsite on the American side of the border, that, even at such a low elevation, was loaded with a foot and a half of fresh snow.

Reasoning that higher up the mountain the accumulation could be double that amount, the buzz for skiing was strong.

Having skied in Haines briefly a few years earlier, I knew the guys who ran the heli operation at the 33-Mile Roadhouse. We woke to perfect blue skies and decided to make a quick drive to 33-Mile to get terrain beta before heading back up Haines Pass with our sleds.

Oskar and I weren't even out of the truck when we heard a voice shout my name from the 33-Mile porch. It was Sean Dog: master of ceremonies, character extraordinaire, and owner of one of the world's best smiles. It was great to see him. Grinning the whole time, he shook with his right hand and handed over a liability waiver form with his left. "You guys could not have picked a better day to get here!" he announced.

It was 8 AM, and the porch was speckled with a handful of pros and clients preparing to jump in the helicopter. With conditions ramping toward perfection, there was sweet excitement in the air.

"Wish we could fly, but we are out of money," I told him reluctantly. "Unfortunately, we're skiing with our sleds up on the pass for today."

We were at the base of the best mountains in the world, on a perfect day, with a helicopter ready to go, but that was the reality of our finances. It pained me to say it, but our trip plans didn't include helicopters, so there were no great expectations.

Sean Dog's smile deflated somewhat. But just then, a figure emerged from the group on the porch. It was Urs, the marketing manager from Mammut, and the greatest supporter of our trip and book project. Out of pure coincidence, Urs was in Haines heli-boarding on his vacation. After some boisterous hellos, he was eager to check out the trucks and campers and learn how our trip had been thus far.

As the grand tour wound down and we had updated him on our breakdowns and triumphs, I playfully asked him "You don't happen to have a little bit extra in the marketing budget for some heli time?"

He laughed it off at first, but as he walked away at the end of our conversation, he said, "You guys must go in the helicopter today."

"But we have already spent all our money. We can't," Oskar responded.

"No, you guys have to go. It's too good today not to. Go, have fun, and invoice me."

"Are you serious?"

"Serious. Have fun," he said laughing, and walked off.

Oskar and I looked at each other as if we had just won the lottery. We did a little dance and ran for our boots. We were about to get in the helicopter. It was a dreamy day, in a dreamlike place, and it was Wednesday.

For heliskiing to truly be the experience it's hyped up to be, you need a number of variables to fall into place. First, amazing terrain. Check. We had the best in the world, complete with fluted peaks, straight-line couloirs, and five thousand-foot powder spines. Second, you need good, stable snow. Check. The conditions were bottomless, light, and safe. Third, no sense of guilt about the cost. Check. For this magical day, it was taken care of. To get the first three in line is a real trick. Getting the fourth—a skilled group that is ready to charge—is the capper. Oskar and I were put in a group with four of the operation's guides. We had a perfect vibe, and everyone was rabid for fresh, technical dream lines.

When all was said and done, it was the best day of skiing of our lives. It was so good that we walked around for two days with indelible grins etched on our faces. The only bad part was telling Gavin and Mark about what they had missed. They were truly happy for us, though, and even as I write this, I still can't help but think about that Wednesday and smile. Thank you, Urs. Hallelujah.

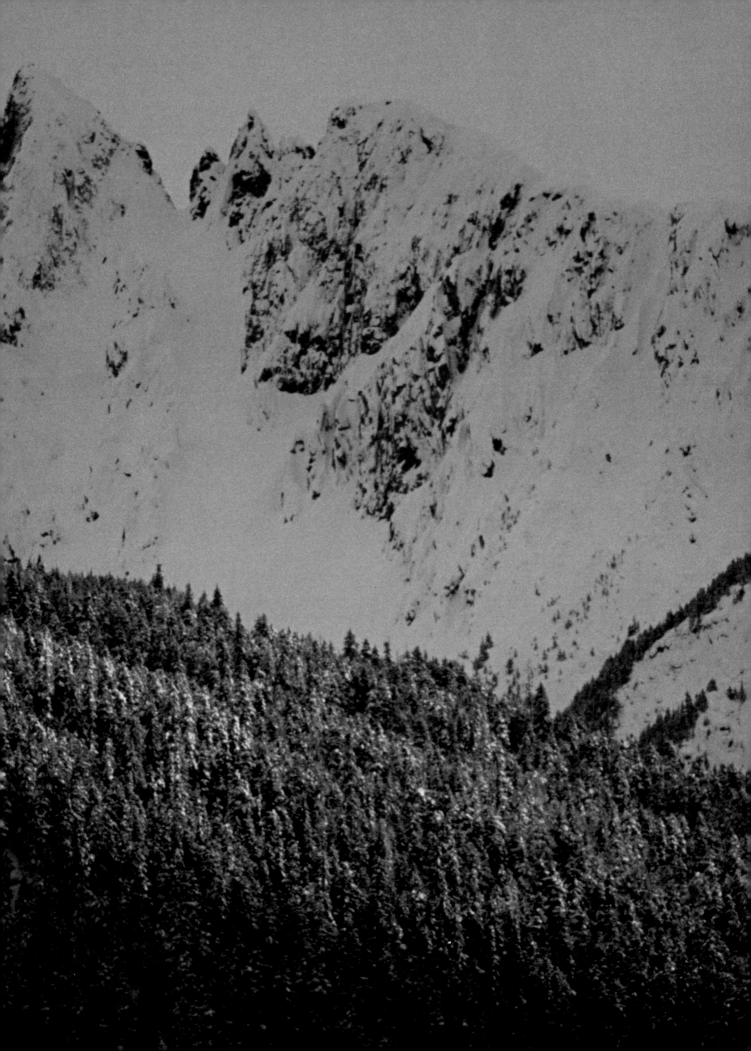

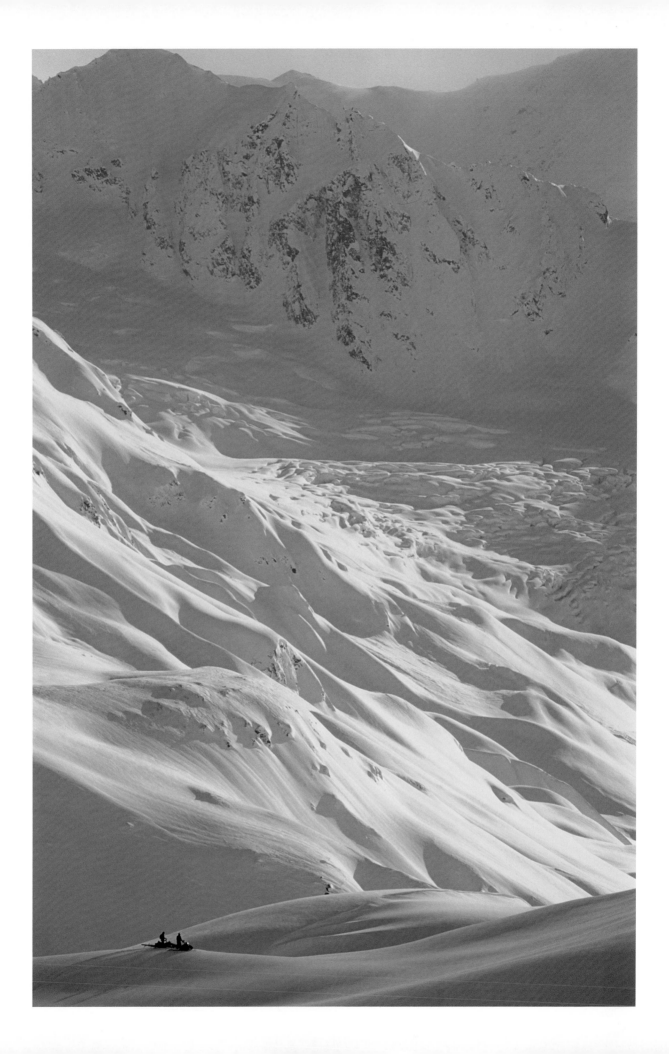

12

THE ALASKAN MYSTIQUE

Next to the tables at the 33-Mile Roadhouse are stacks of magazines. We were eating breakfast one morning and checking out a *National Geographic* that featured a photographic spread of a grizzly bear fighting with a pack of wolves over a moose the wolves had killed. The pictures were amazing, and the article claimed that a duel of this magnitude had never been captured on film before. The four of us were gazing at the photos in amazement when Sean Dog happened to walk by our table. We showed him the photos as if they were something incredible. He took a quick glance, popped his classic wild grin and said, "Oh, I was there for that. I watched that whole thing happen."

"What?"

"Yeah, I sat on the road for eight hours watching it," he said, gums and teeth blazing.

The four of us looked at each other in disbelief.

"Who won?" I asked.

"The wolves got the carcass once the bear was done with it," he said nonchalantly. Then, changing the subject, he added, "It's too bad you guys aren't flying today. It's going to be good...I have to go to the bathroom."

Sean Dog walked off with that grin on his face, and we turned to the last page of the article. There were the wolves, huddled around the fallen moose, with the bear walking away in the distance.

A couple of days later, Gavin, Oskar, and I were hanging out on the porch at 33-Mile when Funny Farm Bruce came up the stairs looking intense. Bruce is a local fisherman and generous character who works with Sean Dog's heli operation. "There's a wounded moose cow down the river," he said. "The wolves have taken a chunk out of her, and they are waiting in the brush for it to get dark. We have permission to take her meat to stock the school's freezer."

He looked over at us, "You guys want to come help?"

"Yes," we all said instantly.

"You guys got guns?"

"No."

"I have to go home and grab a saw."

Bruce then looked over at his wife, who was standing by their truck, and asked her, "Honey, do you have a pistol with you?"

Moving quickly now, and without waiting for her answer, he turned his back to us and walked off the porch. "Let's go, boys."

So we all went by the Funny Farm to pick up a boat, guns, and some sharp knives. We drove down the river in search of the moose, but the sun set before we could locate her on the opposing riverbank. Two days later, driving through the same area, we spotted a swarm of bald eagles feeding on what was now just a bony carcass lying on the sandbar.

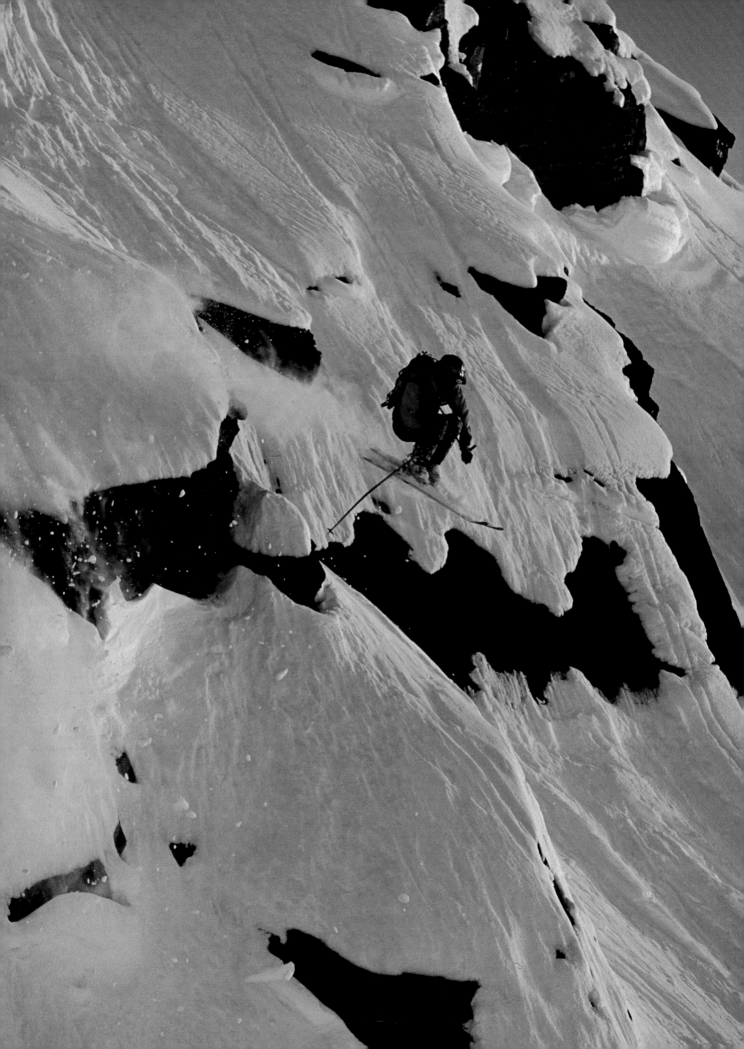

4/14/05
Valdez, AK

Today we went into The Books again. There were five of us, and only four sleds, so Rob and I doubled-up. Two of the three steep uphills were trenched-out so we had to hit them with lots of speed. I like that moment right before you have to commit to the throttle, that quick glance at each other. It might be a mystical notion, but I'm positive the outcome is in the expression. At the base of the first uphill, I looked at Rob, and could tell he was ready to charge. It's wild how a brief exchange like that can converge into a mutual confidence. We pinballed our way to the top; cleared the second but landed in a tree-well; and managed to sail up the off-cambered third.

When we entered The Books, Rob and I set a boot-pack up one of the fins. The ones with names are numbered which seems sort of odd. Since the zone is called The Books, I wish the couloirs were named after novels or authors, not numbers.

Before sunset I watched Stephan ski a death-line. It was 50° plus with a stupid amount of exposure. He skied it as if he were attacking something. It looked brave, strong and fluid. At the bottom, his eyes were euphoric; he was somewhere else, so far gone on that sublime mix of testosterone and adrenaline. The face he skied doesn't have a name. I'm pretty sure Stephan was the first to get it done. We should name it after Conrad because he was bold and it was a bold thing to do. Actually, that face was foreboding as hell. We should call it Heart of Darkness.

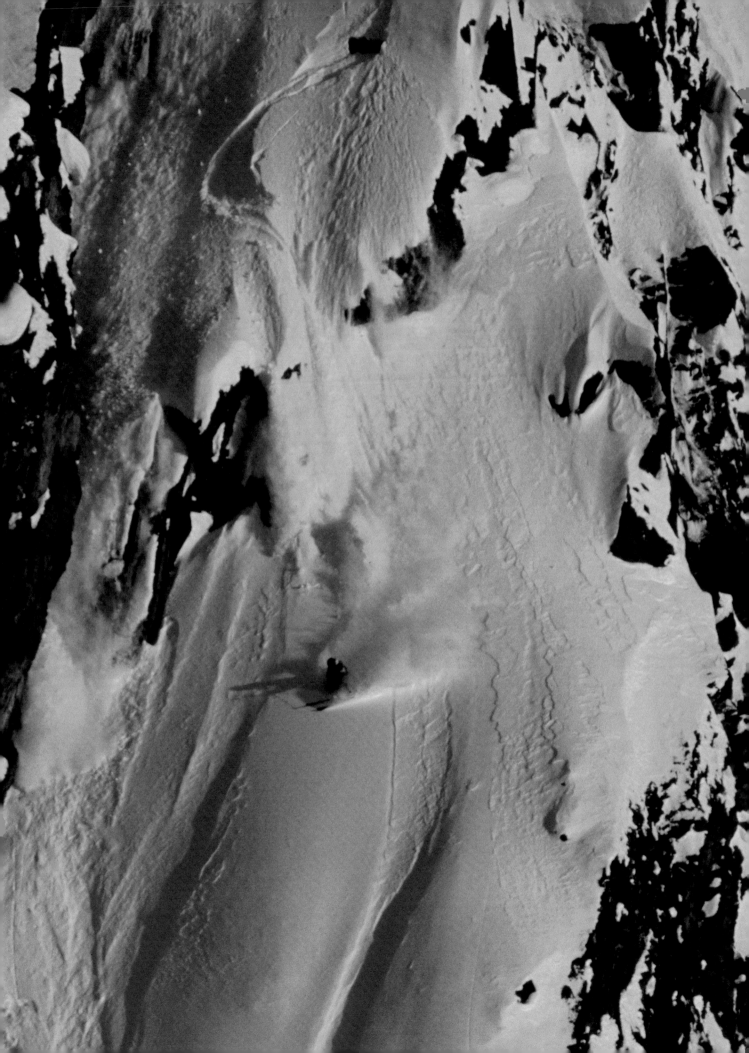

GAS STATION

TO CALL

DIESEL

13

AFTERTHOUGHTS

At the genesis of this trip was the idea of standing atop powdery lines in faraway places without being rushed. We wanted time to buckle our boots or have a laugh with the confidence that six rabid guys weren't skating up the cat track behind us on a hunt for that same line. And with the civilized world in a stew of geopolitical glue, it seemed like a decent time to gain new perspective by exploring the northern mountains.

Powder was the impetus for travel, but now that the journey is complete, it is the travel itself that stands out. Travel was the numbingly beautiful sunsets of the north, the empty mountains unfolding for hundreds of miles beneath our skis, the heated backgammon battles, and the long, meditative miles behind the wheel. Travel was Oskar's lamb chop facial hair period, waking up to the sound of raindrops on the camper's roof, and trying to account for Gavin's whereabouts during a mysterious three-hour nighttime foray in Haines. It was rolling into Valdez for the first time, driving slowly down Hyder's main street so the locals wouldn't blow out our tires with a shotgun, a thermos of warm tea, the sunken feeling of over-extending our budget, and improvising yet another way to configure our gear. Travel was all the friends, family, and generous people we encountered along the road: Glen Wade, Tucker, Shane Spencer, Patrik, Griffin, Slam, Rudy, Philip, Sean Dog, Jeremy, SL1, Che, Pasky, the Whitehorse coffee shop barista, and the Stewart gas station attendant. The list goes on.

It's hard to think of spending too much time at the resort anymore. The core sensation of ski travel stays the same through the generations, but the way we practice it continues to evolve. With the advent of new powder shapes and more efficient modes of travel, it is now possible to arc broad, natural strokes across the canvases of our dreams. As the experience grows more intense, so does the invitation to explore farther and farther afield—another seductive reason to grab some boards and a backgammon set, meet new people, and hit the road in search of wild mountains.

PHOTOGRAHIC INDEX